A Slow Walk through Psalm 119

A Slow Walk through Psalm 119

90 Devotional Meditations

Edward B. Allen

Melbourne

A Slow Walk through Psalm 119:
90 Devotional Meditations
by Edward B. Allen
Copyright © 2018 by Edward B. Allen
All rights reserved worldwide.
Reprinted with revisions, 2020, 2021.

Published by Edward B. Allen
Melbourne, Florida
Email: edward.allen1949@gmail.com

ISBN: 978-1-7320708-0-6 (paperback)
978-1-7320708-1-3 (standard ebook *.epub)
978-1-7320708-2-0 (Kindle ebook *.mobi)

Contact the publisher if you have questions regarding copying this book.

Cover design by Ken Raney (http://kenraney.com).

To Angie

Contents

Contents

Contents

Contents

Preface

The author of Psalm 119 loved the Word of God. Meditating on this psalm yields greater love for the Lord and fresh insight into the ups and downs of life. This book is a collection of devotional meditations, slowly walking through Psalm 119 a few verses at a time. The stories are based on the recollections of actual people and events by friends, family, or myself, unless otherwise indicated. Write your personal thoughts about the passage in the blank space at the bottom of most pages .

The New International Version (NIV) is quoted as the primary translation of the Bible. A word referred to as a word is in *italics*. Cross-references to other Scriptures are in the notes. Scripture references consist of book, chapter, verses, and version (if relevant), for example, "John 3:16 (KJV)" in the King James Version. All titles and scripture references are indexed. Male pronouns are sometimes used to indicate a person of either gender.

I thank my many Facebook friends for their encouraging responses to earlier versions. I am also thankful for the support of my wife, Angie.

E.B.A.

Meditations

1 Blameless

> Blessed are those whose ways are blameless, who walk according to the law of the Lord.
>
> Psalm 119:1 (NIV)

My friend's little ice cream shop was doing quite well. She gave away an ice cream sundae each day to some unsuspecting customer. She was applying the Scriptures about generosity to her business. What makes a business prosper? Of course, offering a good product at a good price is the foundation. A business is successful when it is run honestly, treating customers fairly and employees with respect, kindness, and generosity. Such a business will be sustained, even in hard times.

An upright life, following the Word of God, produces good results. Such a life will be blessed, even in hard times.

PRAYER: Lord, I want to be blessed like my friend's successful business. Amen.

2 Laws of nature

> Blessed are those whose ways are blameless, who walk according to the law of the Lord.
>
> Psalm 119:1 (NIV)

I learned about the laws of nature in science class. I learned about equations like Newton's $F = ma$ and Einstein's $E = mc^2$. Scientists work hard to discover those laws. God invented them. God's laws of nature also include moral laws like "The wages of sin is death"[1] and "Blessed are those whose ways are blameless."

Even though it is impossible for the natural man to live a sinless life,[2] God has provided a way to be free from sin through Jesus Christ. As a result, I have the ability to walk in God's ways. God wants mankind to be blameless, so he can bless. It is one of his laws of nature.

> PRAYER: Lord, I will follow your moral laws which I see in your Word. I want my ways to be blameless. Amen.

PERSONAL THOUGHTS

---

[1]Romans 6:23 (KJV).
[2]Romans 3:23.

3   Seeking

> Blessed are those who keep his statutes
> and seek him with all their heart—they
> do no wrong but follow his ways.
>
> > Psalm 119:2–3 (NIV)

When I was kid, we played hide-and-seek. If Mom
came out, we ignored her, because she was not in
the game. Even if she said, "Dinner's ready!" we
might not notice right away.

The Lord illuminates my mind when I read the
Bible. He prepares circumstances so I can do good
things.[3] Coincidences are not just random events.[4]
The Holy Spirit speaks to my soul. His whispers
and nudges are not just hallucinations. Jesus promised if I will seek the Lord, I will find him.[5] God is
not playing hide-and-seek, but I must be ready to
notice when he is present and active.

> PRAYER: Lord, I am seeking you, and
> listening for your whispers and nudges.
> Amen.

PERSONAL THOUGHTS

---

[3]Ephesians 2:10.
[4]Proverbs 16:33.
[5]Matthew 7:7–8.

4   Fully obeyed

> You have laid down precepts that are to
> be fully obeyed.
>
> Psalm 119:4 (NIV)

I have a regular schedule. I do certain things on Mondays and other things on Tuesdays. The laws of the state are different. The speed limit on the highway is the same every day, during rush hour and late at night when there is no traffic. I don't have the option of choosing when I'll obey the speed limit.

I like to order fish from the menu at restaurants, but I never choose oysters. The laws of the state are different. I must stop at all red lights. I don't have the option of choosing which red light I will obey.

The greatest commandment is "Love the Lord your God," and the second is "Love your neighbor as yourself."[6] I don't have the option of choosing which days of the week I'll obey the greatest commandment. I can't love him on Sunday, and ignore him the rest of the week. I don't have the option of choosing which neighbor to love as myself, and which I'll avoid. I can't choose my favorite verses and be excused from the others.

God's Word is not limited by my schedule. His Word is not a menu from which to pick what I like. God's Word is to be fully obeyed.

> PRAYER: Lord, I want to obey your Word completely. Show me how it applies to me today. Amen.

---

[6]Matthew 22:36–40 (NIV).

5 Steadfast

> Oh, that my ways were steadfast in obeying your decrees! Then I would not be put to shame when I consider all your commands.
>
> Psalm 119:5–6 (NIV)

The mast on a sailboat is steadfast. It always points up. The wire cables that hold up a mast are called *stays*. If the stays are too loose, the mast will flop around in the wind. Something might break.

Prayer is like a spiritual stay. Reading the Word of God is another. Spending time with other Christians is yet another. If the spiritual stays in my life are strong and tight, then I won't flop around. I'll be steadfast, even in stormy seasons.

> PRAYER: Lord, help me to remain steadfast in all of life's stormy seasons. I will tend to all the spiritual stays in my life. Amen.

PERSONAL THOUGHTS

6   Learning

> I will praise you with an upright heart as
> I learn your righteous laws. I will obey
> your decrees; do not utterly forsake me.
> Psalm 119:7–8 (NIV)

The Bible was originally written in languages that I don't understand, over a span of centuries, in different cultures than mine, and in various kinds of literature. I want to obey what the Bible says, but understanding some passages is pretty difficult.

I'm thankful for translators who give me English to read, archaeologists who explain ancient cultures, and commentators who know about literary genres. God brings them into my life as I need them.

When I became a believer, I was not transformed into a super-Christian with complete knowledge of the Bible. Maturing is a learning process. Most of the time, understanding is not difficult. Obeying is what is difficult.

> PRAYER: Lord, help me to understand your Word, so I can put it into practice every day. Amen.

PERSONAL THOUGHTS

7 Purity

> How can a young person stay on the
> path of purity? By living according to
> your word.
>
> Psalm 119:9 (NIV)

As a teenager, this verse taught me that my eyes,
mind, and body must stay pure. As I strived for
purity, Bible study gave me the courage to be different from my peers.

Purity is needed in any area where sin can corrupt. In our oversexualized society, in an era of hy-
peractive hormones, sexual purity is the first kind
that comes to mind. Immorality corrupts marriage,
but obeying the Word has made my marriage wonderful.

Anger, rage, and bitterness corrupt relationships. If the Bible had not taught me about pure
relationships, I would be a bitter cynical person.
I have learned to forgive, to control anger, and
to walk in faith. God has replaced sharp cutting
words with gentle compassionate words.

> PRAYER: Lord, help me to see the path
> of purity and to stay on it. I don't want
> any corrupted relationships. Amen.

PERSONAL THOUGHTS

8   Straying

> I seek you with all my heart; do not let
> me stray from your commands.
>
> Psalm 119:10 (NIV)

Angie hates to see dandelions in the lawn. Dandelion leaves are jagged. Grass is smooth. When a dandelion sprouts, its leaves are hidden under the grass. The yellow flower stands up tall above the green grass and looks pretty. The flower becomes a delicate puff ball. The wind spreads the tiny seeds all over the lawn, so the next generation can sprout. If I don't spray weed killer on them early and often, pretty soon the ugly jagged leaves will be everywhere and empty stalks will dot the landscape.

Straying from the commands of the Lord is like a dandelion in the lawn. Sin hides in the routine of life. At first, it looks pretty and delicate. When it has taken root and spread, its ugly jagged nature becomes obvious to all, and what was pretty and delicate becomes nothing but bare stalks. Sin may try to spread everywhere, but obeying the Word of God is my weed killer.

> PRAYER: Lord, I don't want to stray from
> your Word, or let spiritual weeds sprout
> in my life. Amen.

PERSONAL THOUGHTS

9 Hidden

> I have hidden your word in my heart
> that I might not sin against you.
>
> Psalm 119:11 (NIV)

I went to the hardware store to pick up a few items. When I finished, I found that I had locked my keys in the car with the engine running. I panicked! How could I go home for a key and get back? Then I remembered I had a key hidden in my coin pouch. What a relief. Ahhhh!

I memorized this verse in Sunday School. When I sang Scripture songs, the lyrics lodged in my heart. When I taught a Bible study, I learned more than anyone. Now, like that spare key, the Word is hidden deep inside, ready whenever I need it.

> PRAYER: Lord, I will remember what your Word says, so I will be ready whenever I need it. Amen.

PERSONAL THOUGHTS

10   From God's mouth

> Praise be to you, Lord; teach me your
> decrees. With my lips I recount all the
> laws that come from your mouth.
>
> > Psalm 119:12–13 (NIV)

I took lifeguard training as a teenager. I learned how to swim with my arm around the victim. I learned how to do mouth-to-mouth resuscitation, in case the victim couldn't breathe. You put your mouth over the mouth of the victim and blow. Once you get going with regular breaths, the victim will usually be able to breathe on his own.

Saying God's words out loud is like receiving mouth-to-mouth resuscitation from God. His Word revives my soul. Then I'm able to praise him from the heart.

> PRAYER: Lord, let your Word revive my
> soul, so I can praise you. Amen.

PERSONAL THOUGHTS

11   Great riches

> I rejoice in following your statutes as one rejoices in great riches. I meditate on your precepts and consider your ways. I delight in your decrees; I will not neglect your word.
>
> Psalm 119:14–16 (NIV)

When I was a boy, I enjoyed the story of *Treasure Island* by Robert Louis Stevenson. There was adventure and a treasure map. "X marks the spot."

I also enjoy reading the Bible. Each truth is a treasure. My Bible has a "treasure map," the cross references in the middle column of each page. The truth on one page leads to treasure somewhere else. The concordance in the back of my Bible is the map for word studies, more treasures. There is adventure in finding Bible treasures. The cross references and concordance show where "X marks the spot."

> PRAYER: Lord, I love exploring your Word. Its treasures are precious to me, because they are from you. Amen.

PERSONAL THOUGHTS

12   Meditating and considering

I rejoice in following your statutes as
one rejoices in great riches. I meditate on
your precepts and consider your ways. I
delight in your decrees; I will not neglect
your word.

Psalm 119:14–16 (NIV)

When Angie makes burritos, she lays out the ingredients for the filling: lettuce, tomato, cheese, and
some meat mixed with chorizo and beans. She puts
the flour tortilla on the cast iron griddle. When it's
hot, she puts the fillings in the middle and wraps it
up.

Digesting the Word of God is like eating a burrito. The ingredients of thoughtful meditation and
consideration are wrapped in my joy and delight.
My feelings about the Word are my motivation to
dig deeper with my mind. I devour the Word with
intellect and emotion all wrapped together. No one
disassembles a burrito to eat the ingredients sep-
arately. I won't try to separate the ingredients of
Bible study either. The result is delicious. Yum!

PRAYER: Lord, I love consuming your
Word with both my mind and my feelings. Amen.

PERSONAL THOUGHTS

13   Open eyes

> Be good to your servant while I live that
> I may obey your word. Open my eyes
> that I may see wonderful things in your
> law.
>
> Psalm 119:17–18 (NIV)

I read about the ban-the-bomb movement in high
school. They advocated banning nuclear weapons
world-wide. My reaction was, "They don't understand that all people are sinners. Somebody will
cheat. Simply banning the bomb won't bring peace
on earth." They were assuming that people are nat-
urally good. Even a kid in high school can see that
sin explains much of human behavior. The Bible
makes more sense than ideas like ban-the-bomb.

I read the Bible to understand the world around
me. I pray for fresh insights. God answers my
prayers with wonderful things from the Word.

> PRAYER: Lord, thank you for the in-
> sights into human nature that I learn
> from your Word. Amen.

PERSONAL THOUGHTS

14   Wonderful things

> Be good to your servant while I live, that
> I may obey your word. Open my eyes
> that I may see wonderful things in your
> law.
>
> Psalm 119:17–18 (NIV)

My idea of a balanced meal is "bread and something else." Someone else might say, "Something hot and something cold," or "Dessert and something else." But no matter how much I eat, without good nutrition, I will be hungry all the time.

Unless God opens my eyes, I cannot understand his Word. Without understanding, I cannot obey his Word. Without obedience, I cannot live as a citizen of his kingdom should. Without his Word, my soul will be hungry all the time.

> PRAYER: Lord, guide me as I study the
> Bible, so I can have well balanced nutrition from your Word. Amen.

PERSONAL THOUGHTS

15   Stranger

> I am a stranger on earth; do not hide your commands from me. My soul is consumed with longing for your laws at all times.
>
> Psalm 119:19–20 (NIV)

Songs like "I am a poor wayfaring stranger" and "This world is not my home" speak to my heart. Even though I am a loyal citizen of the USA, I know my eternal citizenship is in the kingdom of heaven. I don't belong to this world's system.

There have been times when there were no true Christian believers around me—in a college dorm, in Army barracks, on the job, and sometimes even in a church. It can feel lonely. Like the psalmist said, "I am a stranger on earth," but I know my eternal citizenship lies in heaven.

> PRAYER: Lord, when I feel like the only Christian, send me your believers for fellowship, and remind me of my eternal home. Amen.

PERSONAL THOUGHTS

16 Arrogance

> You rebuke the arrogant who are accurs-
> ed, those who stray from your com-
> mands.
>
> Psalm 119:21 (NIV)

When I look inside myself, I see my natural self is
arrogant. Except for the grace of God and the in-
fluence of the gospel, I would be a bitter cynic with
a sharp sarcastic tongue. Just because my natural
tendencies lead to an unhappy life, doesn't mean I
am forced to go in that direction. Life with Jesus is
full of "righteousness, peace, and joy."[7]

Jesus taught that the greatest in the kingdom of
heaven is the one who is humble like a child,[8] the
opposite of arrogance. If I'm not watchful, it is easy
to fall back into my natural pattern of arrogance,
thinking that I know better than anybody else.

> PRAYER: Lord, rebuke me when I be-
> come arrogant. Don't let me stray from
> your Word. Amen.

PERSONAL THOUGHTS

---

[7]Romans 14:17 (KJV).
[8]Matthew 18:1–4.

17   Contempt

> Remove from me their scorn and contempt, for I keep your statutes.
>
> Psalm 119:22 (NIV)

I felt excluded from the inner circle of my coworkers. They were having important meetings, but I was not invited. I felt scorned.

C. S. Lewis[9] explained that even if I enter one inner circle, there will always be another inner circle I'm excluded from. This is especially true among unbelievers. They frequently would rather not have a Christian around. Scorn and contempt by unbelievers is normal, but God's love for me means their contempt shouldn't bother me. After all, whose opinion really counts, God's or theirs?

> PRAYER: Lord, help me see the real situation when I feel excluded from an inner circle. Amen.

PERSONAL THOUGHTS

---

[9]C. S. Lewis, "The Inner Ring," *The Weight of Glory and Other Addresses* (Grand Rapids, Michigan: Eerdmans, 1949), 55–66.

18   Meditating

> Though rulers sit together and slander me, your servant will meditate on your decrees. Your statutes are my delight; they are my counselors.
>
> Psalm 119:23–24 (NIV)

In the 1950s, Dad read the newspaper with his morning cup of coffee. In the 1990s, the TV was blaring during breakfast with the latest headline news. Today, I'm reading the news on the Internet while I drink my coffee. Where is time for meditation on the Word of God? I need to rearrange my priorities.

Busy people have a hard time sitting still. Sitting still is the first step for meditation on the Word of God. Even when my body is sitting still, my mind is going "Whir whir whir." I need to quiet my mind and set aside the concerns of the day. I don't have to think about that stuff all the time. My focus is God's truth. Reminding myself about God's love for me, his faithfulness, and his power makes the antics of others shrink and calms my feelings. Then I'm ready for the day.

> PRAYER: Lord, help me to rearrange my priorities to spend more time with you. Amen.

PERSONAL THOUGHTS

19   Slanderers

> Though rulers sit together and slander me, your servant will meditate on your decrees. Your statutes are my delight; they are my counselors.
>
> Psalm 119:23–24 (NIV)

The boss said, "This computer is broken. It never does what I want." He was frustrated. The accountant said, "Can't you make it do everything at the push of a button?" He was overwhelmed with work. Would the next request ask the computer to make coffee in the morning? As the information technology guy, I was the target for complaints.

When I am being harassed by cranky people, God's Word gives me advice. I pray for the right words to respond to them, and for the right attitude. I focus on his Word instead of their words, because his Word gives me life.

> PRAYER: Lord, give me words of peace and reconciliation when those around me are cranky. Amen.

PERSONAL THOUGHTS

20 Sorrow

> I am laid low in the dust; preserve my life according to your word... My soul is weary with sorrow; strengthen me according to your word.
>
> Psalm 119:25,28 (NIV)

When my mother died there was so much to do, funeral arrangements, legal matters, and on and on. I was exhausted. I didn't have time to grieve. I prayed for strength, and the Lord sustained me. Later there was a flood of tears, and God gave me comfort that can't be explained.

Whenever I feel depressed or defeated by circumstances, I can call on the Lord who is the source of life. He preserves me in the face of catastrophe.

> PRAYER: Lord, when I feel defeated and overwhelmed, strengthen and comfort me. Amen.

PERSONAL THOUGHTS

21 Understanding

> I gave an account of my ways and you
> answered me; teach me your decrees.
> Cause me to understand the way of your
> precepts, that I may meditate on your
> wonderful deeds.
>
> Psalm 119:26–27 (NIV)

A starry night sky does not make sense unless I understand who the Creator is. History does not make sense unless I understand that all are sinners and sin oppresses. The fall of a civilization does not make sense unless I understand that idolatry is sin, and its consequence is death. Jesus' death on the cross does not make sense unless I understand both God's justice and God's love for me. God's wonderful deeds do not make sense unless I understand God's righteousness and mercy.

God's righteousness and mercy exposes the corners of my heart. Confession is necessary. I need to learn from him patterns of righteous living, thinking, and feeling. Then I am equipped to obey.

> PRAYER: Lord, teach me your Word. Give me understanding of the world around me and the power to live the way you want me to. Amen.

PERSONAL THOUGHTS

22   Deceitful ways

> Keep me from deceitful ways; be gra-
> cious to me and teach me your law.
>
> Psalm 119:29 (NIV)

Too often I have deceived myself. I look back at
the clumsy insensitive way I treated some of my
friends. Sometimes I have cut off relationships for
no reason. I now realize that my own heart deceived me into thinking I was doing nothing wrong.

Only the Holy Spirit and the Word of God can
cut through my excuses, expose my selfish atti-
tudes, and lead me to repentance. God is gracious
to forgive.

> PRAYER: Lord, expose the times when I
> deceive myself. I want to walk in truth
> all the time. Thank you for forgiving me.
> Amen.

PERSONAL THOUGHTS

23   Faithfulness

> Keep me from deceitful ways; be gracious to me and teach me your law. I have chosen the way of faithfulness; I have set my heart on your laws.
>
> Psalm 119:29–30 (NIV)

I was following the directions of my trusty old GPS. As I approached the Mississippi River, the GPS said, "Bear left onto bridge." I saw barricades, so I went right. As I crossed the new bridge, I saw that the old bridge was gone.

Jesus talked about two roads.[10] The broad road looks good, but leads to destruction. The narrow road leads to life. I will follow the Bible's directions for a kingdom-of-heaven lifestyle instead of taking the broad road to the old bridge and into the water.

> PRAYER: Lord, help me to recognize deceitful ways and to stay on your narrow path of life. Amen.

PERSONAL THOUGHTS

---

[10]Matthew 7:13–14.

24 Running on the path

> I have chosen the way of faithfulness; I have set my heart on your laws. I hold fast to your statutes, Lord; do not let me be put to shame. I run in the path of your commands, for you have broadened my understanding.
>
> Psalm 119:30–32 (NIV)

I was driving along and came to an intersection. I made my turn. I went about a block. "Oh, no! I'm going East instead of West." Embarrassed, I made a U-turn, and backtracked. Then I got back on the right road.

The Holy Spirit convicts me when I turn onto a selfish path. I confess my sin. The confession doesn't mean anything unless I make that U-turn. That is practical repentance. Then I can stay on the road of faithfulness.

> PRAYER: Lord, I choose to stay on the way of faithfulness. Help me remember your Word. Amen.

PERSONAL THOUGHTS

25   Following the way

> Teach me, Lord, the way of your decrees, that I may follow it to the end. Give me understanding so that I may keep your law and obey it with all my heart. Direct me in the path of your commands, for there I find delight.
>
> Psalm 119:33–35 (NIV)

People pursue many lifestyles. Which lifestyle is my favorite? "Lifestyles of the rich and famous" would be nice but expensive. Living the American Dream would be comfortable. Exploring the great outdoors would be refreshing. Life in the big city would be exciting. Sleeping under a palm tree on a tropical island would be carefree.

Like the psalmist, my goal is a godly lifestyle, following the way of God's decrees and the path of his commands. The kingdom-of-God lifestyle is marked by humility and self-sacrificing love for others. It is full of "righteousness, peace, and joy."[11] It may be radical, but it is much better than my other options.

> PRAYER: Lord, I will live your kingdom lifestyle instead of running after a self-centered lifestyle. Amen.

PERSONAL THOUGHTS

---

[11]Romans 14:17 (KJV).

26 Turning

> Turn my heart toward your statutes and
> not toward selfish gain. Turn my eyes
> away from worthless things; preserve
> my life according to your word.
>
> Psalm 119:36–37 (NIV)

When I was learning to drive, I wondered, "How
do I keep the car in the middle of the lane?" If I
asked myself, "Am I too close to the edge?" then
the car would automatically go over there. "Oh!"
I would jerk the steering wheel, and suddenly the
car would be on the other side. Then someone told
me, "Keep your eyes on the middle of the road,
way down there." I was amazed. The car stayed
in the middle and I was hardly moving the steering
wheel.

If I focus on what the Word of God says, then
I will stay in his path, not veering off to the left or
the right. Keeping my eyes on his values, instead of
worthless distractions, will keep me in the middle
of his will for my life, and he will hardly need to
move the steering wheel.

> PRAYER: Lord, help me to stay in the
> middle of your path for my life and to
> ignore worthless distractions. Amen.

PERSONAL THOUGHTS

27 Disgrace

> Fulfill your promise to your servant, so
> that you may be feared. Take away the
> disgrace that I dread, for your laws are
> good. How I long for your precepts! In
> your righteousness preserve my life.
> Psalm 119:38–40 (NIV)

My boss and I had submitted an article for publication in a magazine. The editor rejected it. When I read the reasons, I thought the reviewer was nitpicking. I felt disgraced. A few years later, the editor of another magazine asked us to submit something quickly, so we submitted the rejected article there. That editor loved the article and published it. Disgrace evaporated.

My life should exemplify God's righteousness. He is good to me. The unbeliever makes excuses. "What a coincidence." "How fortunate." "That was lucky." But I know, it is God's hand on my life that takes away disgrace.

> PRAYER: Lord, take away the disgrace
> that the world aims at me for doing your
> will. Amen.

PERSONAL THOUGHTS

28   Unfailing love

> May your unfailing love come to me,
> Lord, your salvation, according to your
> promise; then I can answer anyone who
> taunts me, for I trust in your word.
> Never take your word of truth from my
> mouth, for I have put my hope in your
> laws.
>
> Psalm 119:41–43 (NIV)

Some of the people I have prayed for, including my family, have died from their sickness. Some I've prayed for have been healed, too. At other times, I have seen God's deliverance from sickness even though I didn't know enough to pray at the time. I may not always understand God's ways, but I know he loves people.

Sometimes an atheist will taunt, "Where is your God now?" Sometimes my rational mind taunts me, "Will God show up this time?" But my hope is in the Lord's unfailing love.

> PRAYER: Lord, I know you love me and
> I know you will show up for me when I
> need you. Amen.

PERSONAL THOUGHTS

29   Answering

> I can answer anyone who taunts me, for
> I trust in your word. Never take your
> word of truth from my mouth, for I have
> put my hope in your laws.
>
> Psalm 119:42–43 (NIV)

I met a guy who was on his way to a political de-
monstration. He told me about all of his political
ideas. He kept going on and on. I couldn't respond.
I could tell he was not interested in a discussion.

   Some people try to win an argument by talking
so fast I can't say anything. What they say usually
isn't relevant, didn't make sense, and may not be
true, but God's Word is true. I know God will do
what he says he will do. As long as I cling to God's
Word, I will have an answer.

> PRAYER: Lord, I treasure your Word in
> my heart. I will be ready to answer those
> who don't know you. Amen.

PERSONAL THOUGHTS

30   Freedom

> I will always obey your law, for ever and
> ever. I will walk about in freedom, for I
> have sought out your precepts.
>
> Psalm 119:44–45 (NIV)

I am free. When I'm bored, I am free to turn off the
TV, because the Word of God is fascinating. When
I want to look "cool," I am free to not buy a new
outfit, because God's love for me makes me "cool."
When I'm sad, I am free to not eat comfort food,
because the Holy Spirit comforts me. When I'm
depressed, I am free to not go shopping, because
the Word of God tells me who I am, a child of the
king of the universe. When people around me are
cranky, I am free to love the unlovely, because God
loved me first. I am free from the power of sin, because Jesus died on the cross. I am free to live the
abundant life, because Jesus rose from the dead.

> PRAYER: Lord, thank you for giving me
> true freedom. Amen.

PERSONAL THOUGHTS

31   Speaking before kings

> I will speak of your statutes before kings
> and will not be put to shame, for I de-
> light in your commands because I love
> them. I reach out for your commands,
> which I love, that I may meditate on
> your decrees.
>
> Psalm 119:46–48 (NIV)

In many universities, the faculty and administra-
tion are overwhelmingly atheists and hostile to the
gospel. One doesn't always know how they will react to a Christian testimony.

I was at a university reception. The Dean began
to chat with me. He asked what I would be doing
in retirement. I told him I would be writing Bible
study books. I wondered how he would react. Then
he told me his kids watch Veggie Tales (Christian
cartoon videos). I was relieved to find out he was
sympathetic to the gospel.

Even though I don't expect to talk to kings or
presidents, I need more courage from the Lord
whenever I talk about Christian things with those
in authority above me. If I will step out, the Lord
will make a way.

> PRAYER: Lord, give me courage to speak
> your Word to anyone. Amen.

PERSONAL THOUGHTS

31

32 Hope

Remember your word to your servant,
for you have given me hope. My comfort in my suffering is this: Your promise
preserves my life.

Psalm 119:49–50 (NIV)

We received a postcard that said, "Please come to
Malaysia." My wife and I reacted with "Yes, Lord."
In our hearts, we felt confirmation from the Holy
Spirit. However, we didn't have the money to go
halfway around the world. We began to make plans
to go anyway.

During the next nine months, God provided the
money from an unexpected source. We visited our
friends in Malaysia for about three weeks. I taught
Bible studies during the week at lunch hour, and
preached in a church twice. God gave us hope for
the trip and he fulfilled his promise.

PRAYER: Lord, you are my source of
hope. I know you always fulfill your
promises. Amen.

PERSONAL THOUGHTS

33   Mocked

The arrogant mock me unmercifully, but I do not turn from your law. I remember, Lord, your ancient laws, and I find comfort in them.

Psalm 119:51–52 (NIV)

Even though other students did not mock me to my face, I knew that my lifestyle was very different from their drinking and drugging. By God's grace, I made it through those awkward years with my faith intact.

Like the psalmist, I found hope and comfort in the Word. Knowing his promises sustained me in awkward situations. On the other side of a trial, I can comfort others, because he has comforted me.[12]

PRAYER: Lord, thank you for your comfort in awkward situations. Help me be a comfort to others. Amen.

PERSONAL THOUGHTS

---

[12]2 Corinthians 1:4.

34   Indignation

Indignation grips me because of the
wicked, who have forsaken your law.

Psalm 119:53 (NIV)

The headlines are like a catalog of evil. Around
the world, innocent people are oppressed. Terror-
ists target anyone within reach of a bomb. Murder
and robbery on the streets at home are too common.
Regulations take from the successful and give to the
favored. Laws are passed before anyone can read
what is in them. Enforcement of laws is suspended
if the President doesn't like them. The news is so
outrageous I have to limit my reading to keep my
sanity.

Sin abounds because people have abandoned
the Word of God. I mourn for my country. I mourn
for the world. I find comfort in God's love and in
God's power to redeem. I am eagerly waiting for
the redemption of Planet Earth.

PRAYER: Lord, the world scene gives me
indignation over sin. Give me your compassion when I feel discouraged. Amen.

PERSONAL THOUGHTS

35   Song

> Your decrees are the theme of my song
> wherever I lodge. In the night, Lord, I
> remember your name, that I may keep
> your law. This has been my practice: I
> obey your precepts.
>
>> Psalm 119:54–56 (NIV)

I like to sing. Through the day, I often have a song
about the Lord buzzing in my head. I may be singing songs from church, or I may just make up a
tune. To add some percussion to the music in my
head, I rub my pants in time with the music. Then
my wife says, "Quit rubbing your pants. The noise
is driving me crazy." Then I tell her about the song
in my head. The Word of God in my heart is the
source.

Wherever I happen to be, I am a citizen of God's
kingdom. No matter where I sleep, at home in my
own bed or on a business trip in some hotel, I will
sing of God's love. Whether I am in my daily routine or on vacation, I am looking for ways to obey
the Word.

> PRAYER: Lord, thank you for the joy you
> put in my heart. I will sing your praises
> all day long, out loud or just in my head.
> Amen.

PERSONAL THOUGHTS

36 Face-to-face

You are my portion, Lord; I have promised to obey your words. I have sought your face with all my heart; be gracious to me according to your promise.

Psalm 119:57–58 (NIV)

When I heard that my cousin had moved to nearby Hamilton, Alabama, I made plans to visit him. Except for greetings at a couple of funerals, we hadn't visited in about thirty years. When we met face-to-face, it was as if we had been together just yesterday.

Letters, emails, Christmas cards, and Facebook can't take the place of talking in person. Phone calls and Skype let me hear and see my friend, but they are not the same as a hug.

Conversational prayer is much more than my reading a list to God. For my part, it is honestly telling God how I feel and what I'm thinking. For his part, his Word tells me what he has promised and what he wants me to do. Conversation is two-way communication. Sometimes I feel his hugs, too.

PRAYER: Lord, our two-way conversations are important to me. I promise to obey your Word. Amen.

PERSONAL THOUGHTS

37   Turning my steps

> I have considered my ways and have
> turned my steps to your statutes.
> Psalm 119:59 (NIV)

I have too many decisions to make. Life in the modern world is complicated. I must research all my options, and then figure out which one is best. Which way should I turn my steps? I just need to be decisive.

There is one decision that is more important than the rest. I have decided to obey God's Word. The Word is the criterion that guides all my other decisions. God gave me resolve and will-power, but they are not enough. The power of the Holy Spirit is always there to apply the Word to life's decisions.

> PRAYER: Lord, help me to properly apply your Word to life's decisions. Amen.

PERSONAL THOUGHTS

38   First-time obeyer

> I have considered my ways and have
> turned my steps to your statutes. I will
> hasten and not delay to obey your com-
> mands.
>
> Psalm 119:59–60 (NIV)

A mom with two small boys told one of them to
clean up his mess. He just kept on playing. Her
voice raised a bit, "Are you a first-time obeyer, or
do I have to tell you again?" He jumped into action.

Whether I hear through Bible reading or through
a Holy Spirit nudge, I want to be a "first-time obeyer." God has perfect timing. When he says "Move!"
there is a reason to do it now. Sometimes the Lord
has an appointment for me to help someone. Sometimes he wants to keep me out of trouble.

> PRAYER: Lord, let me hear your voice
> clearly. Help me be a first-time obeyer.
> Amen.

PERSONAL THOUGHTS

39   In a bind

> Though the wicked bind me with ropes,
> I will not forget your law. At midnight
> I rise to give you thanks for your righ-
> teous laws.
>
> Psalm 119:61–62 (NIV)

Around midnight in a college dorm, the guys de-
bated philosophies. The atheist from down the hall
posed an ethical dilemma. "What if such-and-such
happened?" Both courses of action would be sin. I
was in a bind. The atheist thought he had won the
debate.

When I consider the grace and power of God,
I know God can resolve difficult situations in surprising ways. My atheist friend thought divine in-
tervention is an unfair way to win a debate.

> PRAYER: Lord, I thank you for deliver-
> ing me when I'm in a bind. I thank you
> for your overwhelming grace and pow-
> er. Amen.

PERSONAL THOUGHTS

40   Friendship

> I am a friend to all who fear you, to all
> who follow your precepts. The earth
> is filled with your love, Lord; teach me
> your decrees.
>
> Psalm 119:63–64 (NIV)

While on a business trip, I went to Salisbury Cathedral, England. As I was looking at scenes carved on the wall, I noticed the people next to me knew all about those obscure Bible stories. I soon found out they too loved the Lord. They invited me to their home for lunch. About twenty-five years later my wife and I stayed with them for a weekend visit. We've maintained our friendship all these years.

There is an instant bond among those who are in Christ. If someone knows Jesus, I'm already a friend. Such bonds of friendship easily reach across the Atlantic.

> PRAYER: Lord, thank you for instant
> friendships with all those who love you.
> Amen.

PERSONAL THOUGHTS

41   Good judgment

> Do good to your servant according to
> your word, Lord. Teach me knowledge
> and good judgment, for I trust your
> commands.
>
> Psalm 119:65–66 (NIV)

When we were young, my little sister and I got into
arguments. Pretty soon, Mom found out who did
what to whom and then determined who deserved
to sit in the corner for a while. Sometimes the pad-
dle came down off the wall.

Mom learned good judgment from her godly
parents and from studying the Word of God. She
could discern good from evil. Sitting in the corner
taught me a few things. I figured out that studying
the Bible could help me, too.

> PRAYER: Lord, teach me good judgment
> as I study your Word. Amen.

PERSONAL THOUGHTS

42   God is good

Before I was afflicted I went astray, but
now I obey your word. You are good,
and what you do is good; teach me your
decrees.

Psalm 119:67–68 (NIV)

Late at night, a philosophy debate raged down the
hall in the dorm. An atheist challenged a Christian,
"If God is good, why does he allow so much evil in
the world?"

God created the universe and declared it is "very
good,"[13] but sin has consequences—death for per-
petrators and suffering for victims.[14] The death and
resurrection of Jesus has overcome sin, and God's
grace is greater than the suffering caused by sin.
The atheist doesn't know that God is good and that
he is allowing time for repentance.

PRAYER: Lord, thank you for allowing
me time for repentance. I know that you
are always good. Amen.

PERSONAL THOUGHTS

---

[13]Genesis 1:31.
[14]Romans 6:23.

43   Callouses

> Though the arrogant have smeared me
> with lies, I keep your precepts with all
> my heart. Their hearts are callous and
> unfeeling, but I delight in your law.
>
> Psalm 119:69–70 (NIV)

When I play guitar, one hand strums and the other
hand frets the strings. If I haven't played for a
while, the strings seem to cut into my fretting fingers. Ouch! After playing regularly, callouses de-
velop on the tips of my fingers. The callouses are
hard and fretting doesn't hurt anymore.

If I become arrogant, my heart becomes "callous
and unfeeling." But I don't have to be hard and
stoic. The Lord forgives me and drenches me in his
lovingkindness, so my heart becomes soft and compassionate. Then I will forgive others and embrace
the hurting.

> PRAYER: Lord, help me keep my heart
> soft and compassionate, rather than ar-
> rogant and callous. Amen.

PERSONAL THOUGHTS

44   Silver and gold

> It was good for me to be afflicted so that
> I might learn your decrees. The law from
> your mouth is more precious to me than
> thousands of pieces of silver and gold.
>
> Psalm 119:71–72 (NIV)

Every week millions of people buy tickets to the lottery. "Maybe this week I'll hit the jackpot!" Everyone wants to be an instant millionaire. Would I trade a lottery jackpot for my only Bible?

Can the Word of God in my life be measured in dollars and cents? What is the value of having my sins forgiven? Jesus paid for it with his life. What is the value of knowing God loves me? Of knowing what righteous living is? Of having the capacity to love and forgive others? Of having peace in the middle of a personal storm? Of hearing the Holy Spirit speak to my soul and mind? The answer is "Priceless!"

PRAYER: Lord, your Word is priceless to me. Amen.

PERSONAL THOUGHTS

45   Formed by God

> Your hands made me and formed me;
> give me understanding to learn your
> commands. May those who fear you re-
> joice when they see me, for I have put
> my hope in your word.
>
> Psalm 119:73–74 (NIV)

Some people say, "I'm catching a cold." I don't know why anyone would want to catch a cold like a baseball. Right now, my nose is running; my throat itches; I'm coughing; and I generally don't feel good. I would rather say, "I'm fighting a cold." I'm doing all the common-sense things to fight the cold, but I know it is the Lord who heals. Because he is my creator, he knows how my body should work, and he knows it is not working very well right now. Thus, I pray for healing.

Going beyond my physical well-being, he knows my thought patterns. He knows what I understand and what I merely think I understand. The Holy Spirit opens my understanding of the Bible and how it applies to my life. He not only heals my body, but he enlightens my mind.

> PRAYER: Lord, like the psalmist, I pray
> for understanding and wisdom. Please
> heal my body, too. Amen.

PERSONAL THOUGHTS

46   Affliction and comfort

I know, Lord, that your laws are righteous, and that in faithfulness you have afflicted me. May your unfailing love be my comfort, according to your promise to your servant.

Psalm 119:75–76 (NIV)

Everybody has ups and downs in life. Sometimes those around us give us joy or disappointment. The best moments are when I see God working on my behalf. The worst moments are when the consequences of my sin become obvious.

The Lord knows me inside and out, better than I know myself. Through the ups and downs of life, his love comforts me. Some of the downs seem pretty deep, but his Word says he is always faithful toward me.

PRAYER: Lord, thank you for always being there for me through all my ups and downs. Amen.

PERSONAL THOUGHTS

47   Comfort

> I know, Lord, that your laws are righ-
> teous, and that in faithfulness you have
> afflicted me. May your unfailing love be
> my comfort, according to your promise
> to your servant. Let your compassion
> come to me that I may live, for your law
> is my delight.
>
> Psalm 119:75–77 (NIV)

Someone in the office said I had a phone call. When
I got on the phone, the voice on the other end said,
"This is the Palm Beach County Sheriff. Your father is dead." I could hardly believe it. My mother
needed my support, so I wrapped up my affairs and
moved to Florida. About a year later, she passed
away, too. Losing both parents in such a short span
made me feel like an orphan.

The Lord has promised to be a "father to the fa-
therless" and to "set the lonely in families."[15] At
that time, I felt like I qualified. I was slow to let my
feelings come out, but when I let go with a flood
of tears, God was there. My new friends at church
were there like family. When I married, my wife's
family embraced me. The Lord did set this lonely
guy into families.

> PRAYER: Lord, you comforted me when
> I was an orphan. Thank you for putting
> me in families. Amen.

---

[15]Psalm 68:5–6 (NIV).

48 Battles with the arrogant

> May the arrogant be put to shame for wronging me without cause; but I will meditate on your precepts. May those who fear you turn to me, those who understand your statutes. May I wholeheartedly follow your decrees, that I may not be put to shame.
>
> Psalm 119:78–80 (NIV)

Sometimes an office descends into jealousy, gossip, backbiting, factions, jockeying for position, and an occasional stab in the back. At such times, I resort to meditating on the Word of God. Then I realize the day-to-day battles are not very significant. When I think about Mr. So-and-so who could get me fired, I'm reminded that I was looking for a job before I got this one, and God provided for me back then.

Meditating on the Bible helps me see through life's fog, so I do the important things like loving God, loving my enemy, forgiving promptly, comforting the grieving and wounded, speaking the truth, and defending righteousness.

> PRAYER: Lord, thank you for showing me what is really important at the office. Amen.

PERSONAL THOUGHTS

49   Longing

My soul faints with longing for your salvation, but I have put my hope in your word.   My eyes fail, looking for your promise; I say "When will you comfort me?" Though I am like a wineskin in the smoke, I do not forget your decrees.

Psalm 119:81–83 (NIV)

When I finished my degree, I started looking for a job. At first, I looked close to home—rejection letters. I kept on working at the university, but that was not the type of job I had studied for. I broadened the search—more rejection letters. I cried out to the Lord like the psalmist, "My soul faints with longing." Each application was prayerfully sent— more rejection letters and more prayer. After five years, I was offered a job in another state which was right for me.

My hope is in the Lord for all my needs. I cling to his promises in his Word. In due course, he answers. God is faithful.

PRAYER: Lord, you are my hope in the face of rejection. Thank you for providing the right job at the right time. Amen.

PERSONAL THOUGHTS

50   Persecutors

> How long must your servant wait?
> When will you punish my persecutors?
> The arrogant dig pits to trap me, con-
> trary to your law. All your commands
> are trustworthy; help me, for I am being
> persecuted without cause.
>
> Psalm 119:84–86 (NIV)

Angie was about seven years old. One day, as she walked home from school, a little girl attacked her, beat her up, and left her bleeding and crying. Day after day, as Angie walked home from school, the bully was there and Angie came home crying. When an adult friend saw what was happening, she taught Angie to defend herself. It only took one try at self-defense to convince the bully to quit. She never showed up again.

The psalmist, too, faced bullies. He called out to the Lord for help and for justice. Even though they tried to ambush him, his help was from the Lord.

> PRAYER: Lord, when I am confronted by
> a bully, I know that you are there to help
> me. Amen.

PERSONAL THOUGHTS

51 Preserving

> They almost wiped me from the earth,
> but I have not forsaken your precepts.
> In your unfailing love preserve my life,
> that I may obey the statutes of your
> mouth.
>
> Psalm 119:87–88 (NIV)

When I worked for government contractors, I noticed that the engineers who were promoted were those who brought in big new contracts by scheming, lying, deceiving, and flattery. Did I have to give up biblical integrity to get a promotion? What is the path to a successful career? The corporate culture was rewarding greed.

I saw in the Word of God that success in life is marked by persistent obedience, especially following the first two commands, love God and love people.[16] A promotion by a worldly corporation is not the measure of success.

> PRAYER: Lord, I trust you to make a way
> to obey your Word at work. Thank you
> for guiding my career. Amen.

PERSONAL THOUGHTS

---

[16]Matthew 22:37–40.

52 Eternal laws

> Your word, Lord, is eternal; it stands firm in the heavens. Your faithfulness continues through all generations; you established the earth and it endures. Your laws endure to this day, for all things serve you.
>
> Psalm 119:89–91 (NIV)

In high school science class, we learned about the law of gravity, how water is made of hydrogen and oxygen, and how tadpoles grow into frogs. The laws of nature have been the same ever since the universe began.

God established the laws of nature in the beginning. They show how he is faithful and reliable. He has also established his laws regarding righteousness, sin, forgiveness, and redemption. I can trust him and his Word for all my life, and his laws will be the same for generations to come.

> PRAYER: Lord, thank you for being reliable and faithful. I know I can trust you. Amen.

PERSONAL THOUGHTS

53   Not perishing

> If your law had not been my delight, I would have perished in my affliction. I will never forget your precepts, for by them you have preserved my life.
>
> Psalm 119:92–93 (NIV)

When I'm sick, it seems to drag on forever, even if it is actually just a cold. Some of my friends and family have faced chronic health issues that have gone on and on for years.

When the doctors found cancer cells in Faye's lymph nodes, they gave her two years to live. Faye loved Bible study. It was her source of strength year after year as the disease took its toll on her body. She remained cheerful and smiling because she knew who her savior was and the hope found in his Word. Faye lived ten victorious years after the cancer was discovered, rather than two.

> PRAYER: Lord, studying your Word is fun. Thank you for the strength to persevere through times of sickness. Amen.

PERSONAL THOUGHTS

54   Waiting to destroy

> Save me, for I am yours; I have sought
> out your precepts. The wicked are wait-
> ing to destroy me, but I will ponder your
> statutes. To all perfection I see a limit,
> but your commands are boundless.
>
> Psalm 119:94–96 (NIV)

Office politics can be vicious. At my office, gossip
flew. Innuendo crept into conversation. Meetings
erupted with anger. Any little thing became a bat-
tleground. My stomach hurt. The stress pulled at a
hernia in my diaphragm.

The cure for my stomach pain was meditating on the Word of God. In the light of his lovingkindness, office politics faded. The perfection of
his principles made worldly wisdom and cunning
seem trivial and childish. Office politics became just
noise.

> PRAYER: Lord, thank you for show-
> ing me office politics does not matter
> very much. Thank you for showing me
> how to get rid of my stomach pain, too.
> Amen.

PERSONAL THOUGHTS

55 Meditating all day

> Oh, how I love your law! I meditate on
> it all day long. Your commands are al-
> ways with me and make me wiser than
> my enemies.
>
> Psalm 119:97–98 (NIV)

At the office, I'm a busy guy. I've got things to read,
email, letters, and papers to write, people to see,
and meetings to attend. My mind is going "Whir
whir whir." How can I possibly meditate on the
Word of God all day? I'm not in a monastery!

When I look closely at my day, I do walk down
the hall pretty often. I do get a cup of coffee. I do
check my office mailbox. There are many moments
during the day when I can turn my thoughts to a
Bible verse. Even when my mind is focused on the
task at hand, an awareness of God's love warms my
soul. Biblical principles help me understand the
words and actions of people. I guess it's not too
hard to meditate on God's Word all day long, even
on busy days.

> PRAYER: Lord, I will think about your
> Word in all those breaks in the day.
> Thank you for your presence, even
> when I must concentrate on my work.
> Amen.

PERSONAL THOUGHTS

56   Insight

> I have more insight than all my teachers,
> for I meditate on your statutes. I have
> more understanding than the elders, for
> I obey your precepts.
>
> Psalm 119:99–100 (NIV)

While sitting in class, I realized that my high school teacher thought that everyone is born morally perfect, but some are corrupted by society. She didn't know the Bible explains that all are sinners and that sin causes death and destruction. This is why civilizations fall. Knowing the Bible gave me insight in History class.

Any young person who studies and obeys the Bible will have insight into people and human history that worldly teachers will miss. The Word of God opens a person's eyes to see the heart of issues, even though experts are baffled.

> PRAYER: Lord, thank you for your insight into people and society. Thank you for helping me discern good from sin. Amen.

PERSONAL THOUGHTS

57   Paths

> I have kept my feet from every evil path
> so that I might obey your word. I have
> not departed from your laws, for you
> yourself have taught me.
>
> Psalm 119:101–102 (NIV)

When I was looking for my first professional job, a consulting firm sounded like a good opportunity. I found they promise the impossible, and charge too much. Maybe they didn't have biblical business ethics, but they paid very well. A little greed was creeping into my thinking.

We all face temptations to get off the paths of righteousness. It may be letting lust run wild, letting anger erupt, striving for so-called success, or scheming to get rich quick. The Lord has helped me to keep on the right professional path. By studying his Word, I can recognize the lure of the world for what it is, the path to destruction.

> PRAYER: Lord, thank you for guiding me along my career path. Your Word has helped me recognize corporate cultures. Amen.

PERSONAL THOUGHTS

58   Honey

> How sweet are your words to my taste,
> sweeter than honey to my mouth!   I
> gain understanding from your precepts;
> therefore I hate every wrong path.
>
> Psalm 119:103–104 (NIV)

Sticky buns:
   1/2 cup of honey
   1/2 stick of butter
   1/2 cup of chopped pecans
   2 cans of biscuits

Put honey and melted butter in the bottom of a cake pan. Add chopped nuts for the second layer. Place biscuits on top. Bake at 350 degrees until biscuits are brown. While hot, dump biscuits onto a plate. Serve immediately. When my mother made these, there was one more step—lick fingers. The honey made plain biscuits delicious.

The Word of God is also delicious. It feeds my soul with life and puts a sparkle in my eye. It warms my insides with joy and leaves kindness on my fingers. It is so good, I just have to share with others.

> PRAYER: Lord, thank you for your Word.
> It is sweet for my soul. Amen.

PERSONAL THOUGHTS

59   Lights

> Your word is a lamp for my feet, a light
> on my path. I have taken an oath and
> confirmed it, that I will follow your righ-
> teous laws.
>
> Psalm 119:105–106 (NIV)

I've lived in a city all my life. Car headlights shine on the street. Street lights are always on. The house across the street is lit up. If a room is dark, flip a switch.

One night, the power went out. It was really dark. There were no street lights as far as the eye could see. I started groping for a flashlight. "There's one in this drawer somewhere." A squirrel had crept into a substation and shut down the whole town. The squirrel did not survive.

I can't rely on the world to illuminate the right path, or to shine on the truth. Their darkness is normal, and their insight is unreliable. But the Word of God is a sure guide for life and godliness,[17] revealing his will, his righteousness, and his eternal truth.

> PRAYER: Lord, thank you for your guide
> for my life. I know the world's way is
> unreliable. Amen.

PERSONAL THOUGHTS

---

[17]2 Peter 1:3.

60 Willing praises

> I have suffered much; preserve my life,
> Lord, according to your word. Accept,
> Lord, the willing praise of my mouth,
> and teach me your laws.
>
> Psalm 119:107–108 (NIV)

Mom made me go to church. Everyone sang the hymns. I didn't pay much attention. I was more interested in drawing on the bulletin. The songs didn't mean much to me.

Then I asked Jesus into my life. The words of the hymns spoke of God's love and forgiveness that I had experienced. The songs of praise described the wonders of creation that I could see. I started singing, because the song writers' words expressed my thoughts and feelings. I've been singing God's praises ever since.

> PRAYER: Lord, singing your praises has been good for me. I'm looking forward to singing with the heavenly choir through eternity. Amen.

PERSONAL THOUGHTS

61   Snare

> Though I constantly take my life in my
> hands, I will not forget your law. The
> wicked have set a snare for me, but I
> have not strayed from your precepts.
>   Psalm 119:109–110 (NIV)

Temptation is a snare. I tend to blame the devil
for temptation, but much of it comes from myself.[18]
The enemy who sets a snare is me. Selfishness is a
snare. Pride is a snare. Hormones are a snare. There
are many things in life that can be snares.

But yielding to temptation is not automatic. I
don't have to get caught in a snare. The Word of
God shows me the righteous alternative and promises good results when I resist temptation.

> PRAYER: Lord, help me to resist tempta-
> tion, and to see the snares for what they
> really are. Amen.

PERSONAL THOUGHTS

---

[18]James 1:14–15.

61

62   My heritage

> Your statutes are my heritage forever;
> they are the joy of my heart. My heart is
> set on keeping your decrees to the very
> end.
>
> Psalm 119:111–112 (NIV)

Over in the corner is a simple chair with a cane seat
and ladder-style back. A small arrangement of silk
flowers is on the seat, so no one will sit there. The
chair is too fragile. This chair was a wedding gift to
my great grandparents in the 1890s. It is part of my
inheritance.

My favorite photo of my grandmother, Ethel,
shows her reading her Bible. A love for the Bible
is also my inheritance. The Bible at my house is not
just a big book on the coffee table collecting dust. It
is a treasure to be enjoyed every day. Just like my
grandmother, I will read the Word, ponder its mes-
sage, and obey its teaching.

> PRAYER: Lord, thank you for the Bible.
> Reading your Word is a joy. Amen.

PERSONAL THOUGHTS

63   Double-minded people

> I hate double-minded people, but I love
> your law. You are my refuge and my
> shield; I have put my hope in your word.
> Away from me, you evildoers, that I may
> keep the commands of my God!
> > Psalm 119:113–115 (NIV)

"Developing software from requirements is a lot like walking on water. It helps if they're frozen."[19]

I developed a program that generated a daily report for the company president and vice-presidents. Almost every day someone wanted a new feature. Then I would work on the new feature. Sometimes another more urgent request popped up before I finished the last one. Then I would drop everything to add the latest thing. Eventually, the report became so long and complex no one read it.

My focus is on obeying what the Bible teaches. It's not too complex to understand, but it takes the power of the Holy Spirit to follow through. I will press on and not be distracted. The Word of God doesn't have ever changing requirements.

> PRAYER: Lord, thank you for your faithfulness. You are always the same. Help me follow through on what I read in your Word. Amen.

---

[19] Anonymous.

64   Upholding

> Sustain me, my God, according to your promise, and I will live; do not let my hopes be dashed. Uphold me, and I will be delivered; I will always have regard for your decrees.
>
> Psalm 119:116–117 (NIV)

I took swimming lessons at a local pool. Putting my whole face underwater was pretty scary for a six-year old. They wanted me to jump into water over my head! The teacher was out there with her arms open saying, "Come on, jump!" So I jumped. She caught me. I didn't drown after all.

All of us go through trials in life. "How will I ever survive?" It may be sickness, loss of a loved one, living with a difficult person, or working under oppression. The longer it goes, the more hopeless the situation seems. But the Lord gives inner strength to endure. The Lord comforts the grieving when human sympathy is not enough. The Lord works in circumstances to bring relief. The Lord holds me up, so I don't drown after all.

> PRAYER: Lord, thank you for the inner strength to overcome trials in life. Thank you for not letting me drown. Amen.

PERSONAL THOUGHTS

65   Delusion

> You reject all who stray from your de-
> crees, for their delusions come to noth-
> ing. All the wicked of the earth you dis-
> card like dross; therefore I love your stat-
> utes. My flesh trembles in fear of you; I
> stand in awe of your laws.
>
> Psalm 119:118–120 (NIV)

All through high school, people told the boy he was
going to be a star professional basketball player. His
relatives thought he was going to make them all
rich. Relatives tried to cash in on his celebrity, but
he got penalized. He didn't put much effort into
practice or his studies, and eventually was cut from
the team. Greed and arrogance cut short his basketball career.

Unbelievers make big plans, leaving out God's
principles of truth, honesty, and righteousness.
Thinking they will succeed is a delusion.

> PRAYER: Lord, give me your insight, so
> I can recognize the world's delusions.
> Amen.

PERSONAL THOUGHTS

66   Ensuring my well-being

> I have done what is righteous and just;
> do not leave me to my oppressors. En-
> sure your servant's well-being; do not
> let the arrogant oppress me. My eyes
> fail, looking for your salvation, looking
> for your righteous promise.
>
> Psalm 119:121–123 (NIV)

The workman from the power company was suited
up. He was wearing a plastic hard hat, a rubber
jacket, and rubber gloves. He had tools with rubber
coated handles. He was standing in the basket of a
cherry picker. Rubber tubes covered the wires near
him. When hundreds of volts are inches away, it is
important to be well protected.

If I'm working near "high voltage" people, it is
important for me to rely on the Lord for protection.
I can never predict when an angry outburst may
occur. Intimidation may happen at any time. But
the Lord gives me the strength to resist oppression.
His love for me is reliable and guarantees my well-
being.

> PRAYER: Lord, thank you for your pro-
> tection. Give me gracious words when-
> ever I am with "high voltage" people.
> Amen.

PERSONAL THOUGHTS

67   Discernment

> Deal with your servant according to
> your love and teach me your decrees. I
> am your servant; give me discernment
> that I may understand your statutes.
>
> Psalm 119:124–125 (NIV)

Ray taught me three questions to use in Bible study. (1) What does it say? (2) What does it mean? (3) How does it apply to me? Because I don't know Greek, Hebrew, or Aramaic, I rely on Bible translators to find out what the Scriptures say. If the wording of a passage is unclear, I can compare one translation with another. The meaning of most passages is obvious. But sometimes a scholarly commentary is helpful to explain the cultural context, or various interpretations.

How does it apply to me? That is much more difficult. Some things are hard to put into practice, like "Love your enemies."[20] Academic exegesis may be interesting, but the Holy Spirit is the one who gives me the discernment to know what I need to do. That's why I pray as I read the Bible.

> PRAYER: Lord, teach me your Word, so I
> can put it into practice. Amen.

PERSONAL THOUGHTS

---

[20]Matthew 5:43–44 (KJV).

68   Pure gold

> It is time for you to act, Lord; your law is being broken. Because I love your commands more than gold, more than pure gold, and because I consider all your precepts right, I hate every wrong path.
>
> Psalm 119:126–128 (NIV)

For thousands of years gold has been treasured for its beauty. Gold is malleable. One can make gold thread or very thin gold leaf. Gold is easy to make into jewelry, and does not tarnish. It's perfect for wedding rings. My wife and I had just gotten engaged when we went shopping for gold wedding rings. We bought the first pair we tried on. They fit perfectly. They are precious symbols of our marriage.

Even though gold is rare and expensive, like the psalmist, I treasure the Word of God even more. Gold cannot tell me how to live righteously.

> PRAYER: Lord, thank you for your Word which tells me how to live and how to avoid going down a wrong path. Amen.

PERSONAL THOUGHTS

69   Unfolding

> Your statutes are wonderful; therefore I obey them. The unfolding of your words gives light; it gives understanding to the simple.
>
> Psalm 119:129–130 (NIV)

The mailbox had a letter. When I opened the envelope, I saw that the letter had been folded twice to fit the envelope. I had to unfold the letter to read it.

The Word of God is like that folded letter. If I will obey what it says, then I will experience good results. Seeing the good results will give me more understanding of the Word than a bookshelf of theology books. Understanding the Word in this way is available to everyone, irrespective of one's education.

PRAYER: Lord, help me unfold your Word. I want to understand how it applies to me. Amen.

PERSONAL THOUGHTS

70 Directing my footsteps

> I open my mouth and pant, longing for your commands. Turn to me and have mercy on me, as you always do to those who love your name. Direct my footsteps according to your word; let no sin rule over me.
>
> Psalm 119:131–133 (NIV)

I was on a business trip. The weather in Cleveland was cold, but it wasn't snowing. As I drove into Ashtabula County, it started snowing. My appointment was out in the country. It was dark when I headed to the hotel. I must have made a wrong turn. Alone and without any way to communicate, I ended up stuck on an icy road. When I spun the tires, the car slipped sideways toward a steep hill on a side street. I said to myself, "Let's not do that anymore." I prayed for creative ideas. How could I get past that icy patch? The Lord answered my prayer as I chipped away at the ice, and I got to the hotel safely.

When I feel alone, the Lord is there. He responded to my cry for mercy and showed me what to do. He reminds me I am never really alone.

> PRAYER: Lord, thank you for always being with me. Thank you for your mercy. Amen.

PERSONAL THOUGHTS

71   Tears

> Redeem me from human oppression
> that I may obey your precepts. Make
> your face shine on your servant and
> teach me your decrees. Streams of tears
> flow from my eyes, for your law is not
> obeyed.
>
> Psalm 119:134–136 (NIV)

When I learned that two of my church friends were
in an immoral relationship, I had a knot in the pit of
my stomach from grief. People in the world sin all
the time and no one is surprised, but I'm grieved
when Christians don't live according to the Word
of God. I rejoice when they repent. Sin has bad
consequences which I want loved ones to avoid.

The blood of Jesus cleanses us from sin. Forgiveness is just a prayer away. God can redeem, even as
the consequences of sin play out.

> PRAYER: Lord, thank you for forgiving
> my sins. I pray you will bring my friends
> in immoral relationships to repentance.
> Amen.

PERSONAL THOUGHTS

72 Righteousness and truth

> You are righteous, Lord, and your laws
> are right. The statutes you have laid
> down are righteous; they are fully trust-
> worthy.
>
> Psalm 119:137–138 (NIV)

The witness came forward. The court clerk said, "Raise your right hand," and then said, "Do you solemnly swear that you will tell the truth, the whole truth, and nothing but the truth, so help you God?" Truth is the foundation of justice. Without truth in the courtroom, justice is perverted. If a witness suppresses the truth, then the guilty may go free or the innocent may suffer. If the judge or jury ignores the truth then justice is corrupted.

The Lord knows the whole truth, and he says nothing but the truth. The Father is well aware of all my sin. He also is merciful, and so he provided a way for me to be forgiven. His justice is based on the truth, and his mercy is based on the truth as well. The Lord is the righteous and true judge.

> PRAYER: Lord, thank you for your jus-
> tice and mercy. Help me to always live
> truthfully. Amen.

PERSONAL THOUGHTS

73 My zeal

My zeal wears me out, for my enemies ignore your words. Your promises have been thoroughly tested, and your servant loves them.

Psalm 119:139–140 (NIV)

One of my tasks at work was to write proposals for government contracts. I was very careful to make sure whatever we were promising was something we could do and would do. My colleagues, who were more senior than I, would edit what I wrote. They made the proposal sound like we were miracle workers who could "jump over the moon." In my zeal, I had some heated arguments with them. I came home worn out by the battles.

Those who don't believe the Word of God will keep on acting selfishly. My coworkers were more concerned about getting caught than being honest. They didn't realize that conducting business honestly will bring good results. I guess my zeal was not convincing.

PRAYER: Lord, give me your wisdom for dealing with dishonest people. I love the truth. Amen.

PERSONAL THOUGHTS

74   Despised

Though I am lonely and despised, I do not forget your precepts. Your righteousness is everlasting and your law is true.

Psalm 119:141–142 (NIV)

I was guest speaker at a Bible study in an office building in Kuala Lumpur, Malaysia. This small group of believers used their lunch hour to meet. Some of the ladies had husbands who were Buddhists or Hindus and would not let them attend church. Some had to keep their faith a secret from their families. A lunch-time meeting was their only opportunity for Christian worship, Bible study, and fellowship. Even though their faith was despised at home, they were eager to study God's Word. Their faith is a vivid example of persistence and steadfastness.

PRAYER: Lord, help me be persistent and steadfast like those ladies whose faith was despised by their unbelieving husbands. Amen.

PERSONAL THOUGHTS

75   Delight

> Trouble and distress have come upon
> me, but your commands give me de-
> light.   Your statutes are always righ-
> teous; give me understanding that I may
> live.
>
> Psalm 119:143–144 (NIV)

I was ten years old at Bible camp. The preacher
asked anyone who had never asked Jesus to come
in to stand up. I couldn't remember doing that, so I
sort of stood up. The guys down the bench were encouraging me. After the service a camp counselor
talked with me and I confessed my sin and asked
Jesus into my life. As I went back to the cabin, I felt
like I was walking on clouds. I was overjoyed.

Whenever I meditate on the grace of God, I feel
the same delight as that first night. Trouble and dis-
tress come to everyone from time to time, but his
grace and truth are on the inside of me where the
storms on the outside cannot touch my equilibrium.

> PRAYER: Lord, thank you for your sal-
> vation. Thinking about it fills me with
> delight. Amen.

PERSONAL THOUGHTS

76 Crying out

> I call with all my heart; answer me, Lord,
> and I will obey your decrees. I call out
> to you; save me and I will keep your
> statutes. I rise before dawn and cry for
> help; I have put my hope in your word.
>
> Psalm 119:145–147 (NIV)

During the Vietnam war, there was a lottery to determine who would be drafted into the Army. I got a low number. I was guaranteed to get drafted. My peers were going to Vietnam and coming home in body bags. I dreaded the thought of killing someone in combat, and I certainly didn't want to end up in a body bag. So, I cried out to the Lord.

Through a series of providential circumstances my induction into the Army was delayed, and consequently, I never went to Vietnam. To my surprise, the job I was assigned in the Army was a stepping stone to my career later.

My hope was in the Lord, and he was faithful to guide my life. I know I can call on him anytime about anything. My hope is in him.

> PRAYER: Lord, thank you for answering my cries, preserving my life, and guiding my career. Amen.

PERSONAL THOUGHTS

77   Time to meditate

My eyes stay open through the watches
of the night, that I may meditate on your
promises. Hear my voice in accordance
with your love; preserve my life, Lord,
according to your laws.

Psalm 119:148–149 (NIV)

The psalmist liked to meditate on the Scriptures late
at night. It's quiet. There are no distractions. When
I was in college, I found if I tried to read my Bible
and pray late at night, I would fall asleep.

Early in the morning worked much better for
me. The alarm clock went off. I took a shower to
wake up. I got cleaned up and dressed. Then I
was ready to receive what God had to say to me.
I read, meditated, and prayed. Each person has to
find his own time and place in the day or night that
allows meditation on the Word of God without distractions.

PRAYER: Lord, thank you for your Word.
Show me the best time to read, meditate,
and pray every day. Amen.

PERSONAL THOUGHTS

78   Near

> Those who devise wicked schemes are
> near, but they are far from your law. Yet
> you are near, Lord, and all your com-
> mands are true. Long ago I learned from
> your statutes that you established them
> to last forever.
>
> Psalm 119:150–152 (NIV)

Some people think God created our world like a
watchmaker, and then went away to the other side
of the universe. Some people think he comes back
to visit on holidays, like Christmas, Easter, and
Mother's Day. Some people think God just visits
church buildings on weekends. Some people think
God lives at the church building, and they visit him
on Sunday morning, Sunday evening, and Wednes-
day night.

God is near when I hug a friend I see at the gro-
cery store, and when I pray for the stranger in aisle
five who is hurting. The Lord is with me through-
out the day at the office, and when I play guitar in
the living room at home. God is near all the time.
He has promised to be near forever.

> PRAYER: Lord, thank you for being very
> near to me. Amen.

PERSONAL THOUGHTS

79   My cause

Look on my suffering and deliver me, for I have not forgotten your law. Defend my cause and redeem me; preserve my life according to your promise.

Psalm 119:153–154 (NIV)

I was working at a university. Keeping my job depended on a stream of research grants to pay my salary. At the same time, my wife Angie was self-employed. Her income depended on a steady stream of customers. We had to rely on the Lord to provide for us. Whenever we submitted a research proposal, my boss, who was Muslim, would say, "Ask Angie to pray that the proposal will be accepted." He knew about the power of prayer.

Like the psalmist, we prayed, "Defend my cause," because we knew about the power of prayer, too.

PRAYER: Lord, thank you for providing for me in the past. Defend my cause today, too. Amen.

PERSONAL THOUGHTS

80 Seeking answers

> Salvation is far from the wicked, for they
> do not seek out your decrees. Your com-
> passion, Lord, is great; preserve my life
> according to your laws.
>
> Psalm 119:155–156 (NIV)

"What does the Bible say about that?" When this
question comes up, I swing into action! The cross
references in the middle column of my Bible might
lead to the answer. When I don't know where to
start, I turn to the concordance in the back of my
Bible. A word study can turn up treasures. When
English words are not enough, a Hebrew and Greek
concordance may give that extra nuance of insight.
When a verse is hard to figure out, a commentary
may have the answer—or maybe not.

I love to search the Scriptures. They explain the
way of salvation. They show what kingdom living
is about. They let me know that God loves me and
that he has compassion on his children.

> PRAYER: Lord, the truths of your Word
> are like treasure. Help me to find your
> answers to life's issues. Amen.

PERSONAL THOUGHTS

81 Faithless people

> Many are the foes who persecute me, but
> I have not turned from your statutes. I
> look on the faithless with loathing, for
> they do not obey your word.
>
> Psalm 119:157–158 (NIV)

I encounter many who don't try to obey the Bible. A modern lifestyle ignores biblical ethics. Most of them don't profess any faith at all. Some go to church just for show. It's disappointing, but not surprising.

Just because the faithless live selfish lifestyles is no excuse for me to turn away from the path of life. I'm determined to do what the Bible teaches. The rewards are amazing.

> PRAYER: Lord, even though many around me don't trust you, I will. I believe your Word and I will obey it. Amen.

PERSONAL THOUGHTS

82   True words

> See how I love your precepts; preserve
> my life, Lord, in accordance with your
> love. All your words are true; all your
> righteous laws are eternal.
>
> Psalm 119:159–160 (NIV)

When we got a new washing machine, it included
an instruction manual. I expected the manual to tell
the truth. I wondered what a knob was for, so I
looked in the manual for an explanation. Oops—
the picture in the manual didn't have that knob.

Human words can be mistaken or obsolete, but
God's words are true and eternal. The truth of the
Scriptures is a reflection of God's character. Like an
instruction manual for life, the Scriptures are true,
given by a God who is completely honest.

> PRAYER: Lord, thank you for the truths
> of the Bible. They are always up to date.
> Amen.

PERSONAL THOUGHTS

83   Speaking truthfully

> See how I love your precepts; preserve
> my life, Lord, in accordance with your
> love. All your words are true; all your
> righteous laws are eternal.
>
> Psalm 119:159–160 (NIV)

I wondered why traffic was heavy near the airport.
It turned out that a candidate for President was
about to have a rally there. After his speech, those
in the news media were spinning what he said.
Those for him had compliments; those against him
had criticism.

Spinning the truth and outright lying is the
world's way of manipulating listeners. I can't talk
that way anymore. I must live openly without pre-
tending but speaking truthfully.[21] As I grow spir-
itually, I am learning to speak the truth in love.[22]
When I do, those listening will be encouraged, comforted, and built up.

> PRAYER: Lord, help me to always speak
> truthfully with love toward those listen-
> ing. Amen.

PERSONAL THOUGHTS

---

[21]Ephesians 4:25.
[22]Ephesians 4:15.

84   Rejoicing

Rulers persecute me without cause, but my heart trembles at your word. I rejoice in your promise like one who finds great spoil. I hate and detest falsehood, but I love your law.

Psalm 119:161–163 (NIV)

In ancient times, whenever an enemy was defeated, the victors claimed the belongings of the vanquished as *spoil*. For example, Israel's capital city Samaria was besieged by Aram (Syria).[23] The siege was mysteriously lifted by the Lord. Four men with leprosy found the Aramean camp abandoned. They and the people of the city claimed the unexpected spoil and rejoiced. The Lord had delivered them.

Like the psalmist, I rejoice when I see a promise in the Bible that applies to me. One of my favorite promises is Jesus promised to be with me through the Holy Spirit until he returns to earth.[24] It makes me happy, like finding unexpected treasure.

PRAYER: Lord, I rejoice when I find one of your promises in your Word. Thank you for your presence through the Holy Spirit. Amen.

PERSONAL THOUGHTS

---

[23]2 Kings 6:24; 7:3–20.
[24]Matthew 28:20.

85 Peace

> Seven times a day I praise you for your
> righteous laws. Great peace have those
> who love your law, and nothing can
> make them stumble.
>
> Psalm 119:164–165 (NIV)

Some people think that *peace* is the absence of noise.
If you go to a remote place you will have that kind
of peace. The most peaceful place on earth must
be the anechoic chamber over at the university's
acoustics lab. The walls, floor, and ceiling of the
room are covered with thick insulation that absorb
all sounds. Sounds from outside can't get in and
sounds inside can't reverberate. There is no noise—
peace.

Some people try to have a peaceful life by creat-
ing a noise-free environment. Others seek a peaceful inner life through yoga or some Eastern religion.
These don't really satisfy.

True inner peace belongs to those who love the
Word of God. The peace that passes understanding[25] is a gift from God. When I experience God's
peace inside, noise from the outside doesn't upset
me. His peace inside calms my fears and evapo-
rates confusion.

> PRAYER: Lord, thank you for your peace
> in my soul. It is amazing. Amen.

---

[25]Philippians 4:7 (KJV).

86   Following instructions

> I wait for your salvation, Lord, and I follow your commands. I obey your statutes, for I love them greatly. I obey your precepts and your statutes, for all my ways are known to you.
>
> Psalm 119:166–168 (NIV)

I bought a kit to make closet storage. The box said, "Some assembly required." When I opened the box, there were all these precisely cut pieces, a small bag of screws, and a folded piece of paper, the manufacturer's instructions. I have learned the hard way how important those instructions can be. When I don't pay attention to them, the pieces don't fit; something gets put in backwards; and when I'm done, I say, "I wonder what these extra parts are for."

When I try to put together the pieces of my life, it helps to follow the "manufacturer's instructions." The Lord created me. He knows me inside out, better than anyone. His Word tells me how to live. When I obey, the pieces of my life fit together perfectly.

> PRAYER: Lord, thank you for showing me that obeying your Word is how to fit together the pieces of my life. Amen.

PERSONAL THOUGHTS

87   Asking for understanding

> May my cry come before you, Lord; give me understanding according to your word. May my supplication come before you; deliver me according to your promise.
>
> Psalm 119:169–170 (NIV)

After twenty years working an 8-to-5 job, I went back to school. Being a student again was culture shock. There I was, facing a big exam. Some of the topics I was studying I had never had in class. Some of the theory didn't make much sense to me. I felt intimidated.

The Bible says, "If any of you lacks wisdom, you should ask God."[26] So I did—over and over. When exam day came, I did the best I could. I passed—barely. I was happy and thankful!

The Lord is my source of wisdom and understanding. When I ask him, he responds.

> PRAYER: Lord, thank you for giving me understanding whenever I ask for it. Thank you for delivering me. Amen.

PERSONAL THOUGHTS

---

[26]James 1:5 (NIV).

88   Singing the psalms

May my lips overflow with praise, for you teach me your decrees. May my tongue sing of your word, for all your commands are righteous.

Psalm 119:171–172 (NIV)

The padded envelope arrived in the mail. When Faye opened it, she found a cassette tape from her twin brother Ray. As she listened to Ray's voice sharing news about the family, she felt like she was sitting at his breakfast table. Ray read from the Bible, shared a devotional thought, and sang a psalm. He had a psalter that his grandfather had used over a hundred years ago. The text of each psalm was labeled with the name of a tune. Ray sang the words of the psalm according to that tune. Ray and Faye loved the Word of God and could share a moment of worship even though they were separated by a thousand miles.

PRAYER: Lord, I will sing your praises and the words of the psalms will help me. Amen.

PERSONAL THOUGHTS

89   Help

> May your hand be ready to help me, for
> I have chosen your precepts. I long for
> your salvation, Lord, and your law gives
> me delight.
>
> Psalm 119:173–174 (NIV)

We had moved into the neighborhood a short time
ago. Some baseboards had water stains, so I wanted
to replace them. However, I didn't have any tools
to pry them loose. I prayed for a way to do this
project.

When I told the young man next door about my
project, he immediately replied, "You can borrow
my tools. I used to work on flooring. I have all
kinds of tools." He loaned me a couple of tools.
The baseboards popped right off without scarring
the wall. The Lord answered my prayer through
the help of a neighbor whom I barely knew.

> PRAYER: Lord, thank you for sending
> helpers for my projects. I know my re-
> sources are limited, but yours are abun-
> dant. Amen.

PERSONAL THOUGHTS

90   Praises

> Let me live that I may praise you, and
> may your laws sustain me.   I have
> strayed like a lost sheep. Seek your ser-
> vant, for I have not forgotten your com-
> mands.
>
>   Psalm 119:175–176 (NIV)

It was a quick dinner, because we had things to
do. I set up folding chairs in the living room as
my wife cleaned up the kitchen. I tuned the guitars
and turned on the porch light. The kitchen smelled
like the cake that had come out of the oven. Before
long, the driveway filled up with cars, and the living room filled with singing.

Singing praises helps me forget about the distractions of life and focus on the Lord. I can play
guitar and sing by myself, but worshiping with
friends in a living room is even better.

> PRAYER: Lord, I will praise you from my
> heart all my days. Send me other wor-
> shipers, so we can praise you together.
> Amen.

. . . .
Please write a brief review of this book and post it
at your on-line bookstore(s).

If you want to receive a weekly devotional meditation, please send your email address to me at
edward.allen1949@gmail.com
Your email will not be used for any other purpose.

Index

About the author

Edward B. Allen is the author of these books in daily devotional format.

- *A Slow Walk through Psalm 119: 90 Devotional Meditations*

- *A Slow Walk with James: 90 Devotional Meditations*

- *A Slow Walk with Peter: 275 Devotional Meditations*, including meditations on Jude

- *A Slow Walk during Christmas and Easter: Devotional Meditations for Advent and Lent*, including a chronological paraphrase of the Scriptures

He is also the author of these other books which are straight reads with a devotional slant.

- *The Kingdom of Heaven: A Devotional Commentary on the Discourses of Jesus in Matthew*

- *Revelation: A Devotional Commentary*, including illustrations by Albrecht Dürer, fifteen meditations, and questions for personal or group study

- *Under the Sun and in the Kingdom: A Devotional Commentary on Ecclesiastes*

- *Love, Sex, Money, and Power: A Devotional Commentary*, including twelve meditations

- *Honest Questions: A Personal Commentary on Genesis 1 through 11*

He has led discussion Bible-study groups in evangelical churches for over 45 years, and has authored devotional articles for *The Upper Room* and *The Secret Place* magazines. He received a Ph.D. in Computer Science degree at Florida Atlantic University. He has had a career in software engineering and has authored or coauthored over 80 professional papers.

Made in the USA
Columbia, SC
14 November 2024

46401107R00061